Hello & welcome!

I am so glad you're here.

The intention of this cook book is to provide you with approachable, nourishing recipes for you to enjoy during your gut healing process and beyond. Made with gut-nourishing ingredients, these recipes are designed to be acid reflux-friendly, meaning they do not include common acid reflux "triggers" (tomatoes, spicy flavors, chocolate, peppermint, etc). However, please note that <u>everyone has unique dietary needs</u> and that food is often not the root cause of IBS/acid reflux symptoms. If you have questions related to your specific nutrition needs, please contact our team at info@mollypelletier.com.

It is my hope that these recipes are enjoyable for you to create and consume. Remember, our bodies (and digestive systems) need adequate, consistent nutrition in order to function and thrive. Let's bring back the joy in nourishing our bodies and minds.

With love,

Molly

The Flora Philosophy:

FOOD SHOULD BE FUN.

I'd love for you to think of this cookbook as a starting point for your own creations in the kitchen. Use the recipes and ideas as a base, then feel free to add your own spin!

Look for the icon: *Prep-ahead!* for time-saving meal prep options

---

Disclaimer: The information in this book/meal plan is in no way prescriptive or advisory, FLORA KITCHEN and content by Molly Pelletier does not intend to replace medical advice, psychological advice, or personalized Nutrition Therapy. The reader assumes full responsibility for consulting a qualified health professional regarding health conditions or concerns, and before starting a new diet/exercise/wellness program. Molly Pelletier and accompanying social media are not responsible for adverse effects/reactions resulting from the use of any recipes, plans or suggestions herein or procedures undertaken hereafter. If you are experiencing gastrointestinal discomfort/symptoms, have a medical condition, food allergy, or history of an eating disorder, please seek help from a qualified medical professional.

10 Tips for
ACID REFLUX PREVENTION

1. Find ways to help yourself manage stress <u>daily</u>.

2. Aim for 3 meals with 1-2 snacks (vs 2 large meals). Incorporate a variety of foods to support a diverse, healthy gut microbiome.

3. Honor hunger and fullness cues. Don't wait until you are starving to eat.

4. Avoid laying down or slouching 2-3 hours after eating.

5. Chew food well to aide the digestion process.

6. Take 5-7 deep breaths before your meal to relax the abdomen, decrease stress, tap into the Rest & Digest response.

7. Drink liquids outside of meal times to avoid diluting digestive enzymes (avoid exceeding 8oz of liquid during meals).

8. Encourage healthy bowel movements by eating adequate carbohydrates and fiber, and incorporating gentle movement (walking, yoga, etc).

9. Be mindful of caffeine, carbonation, and alcoholic beverages. If you choose to consume, enjoy in moderation.

10. Always have food before caffeinated drinks such as coffee or tea.

References on p. 898

KITCHEN STAPLES

A few items I always have on hand

Pantry

- white rice, wild rice, quinoa
- pasta and legume-based pasta
- bone broth or other broth
- oats (blend or process for oat flour)
- whole grain bread or sourdough bread
- whole grain crackers
- tortillas
- chia seeds, flax meal, hemp hearts
- cashews, walnuts, pumpkin seeds
- tahini, sunflower seed butter, almond butter
- reflux-friendly seasonings (see next page)
- vanilla protein powder or collagen powder
- avocado oil, extra virgin olive oil, garlic-infused olive oil

Fridge

- greek yogurt or non-dairy alternative
- fruit such as melons, bananas, and plums
- vegetables such as broccoli, carrot, zucchini
- eggs, liquid egg whites
- tofu, tempe
- cheese or nondairy cheese alternative

Freezer

- edamame beans
- turkey or chicken burgers
- shrimp, salmon fillets
- frozen veggies such as brussel sprouts, mushrooms, artichoke
- frozen fruit such as strawberries and bananas

Kitchen Tools

- nontoxic, nonstick pan
- high-speed blender or food processor
- sharp knives, cutting board
- silicone muffin tin and silicone donut mold
- vegetable peeler (or spiralizer)

REFLUX FRIENDLY SEASONINGS

Basil
Thyme
Turmeric
Sea salt or table salt
Flaky Maldon salt
Rosemary
Fennel
Celery Seed
Oregano
Parsley
Cilantro
Dill
Bay Leaf
Nutritional Yeast
Za'atar seasoning
Cinnamon (<1 tsp/serving)
Garlic-infused olive oil

Garlic/onion (raw or powder), black pepper, ginger, and lemon juice may not be a trigger for every person with reflux. **Use or omit as tolerated.**

(You can use fresh or dried herbs)

5-DAY MEAL PLAN
for meal ideas & inspiration

	Breakfast	Snack	Lunch	Dinner
Day 1	Spinach Egg White Feta Bites (p. 9) + whole grain toast w/ sunflower seed butter	2-3 Carrot Cake Bites (p. 28)	High Protein Butternut Squash Pasta (p. 64)	Salmon Rice Bowl (p. 45)
Day 2	Whole Grain French Toast Sticks (p. 8) topped w/ greek or dairy-free yogurt + sunflower seed butter	Oat & Seed Bar (p. 24) + 1 cup cantaloupe or other fruit	5-Minute Avocado Egg Salad Sandwich (p. 35) + sliced cucumbers + Carrot Cake Bite (p. 28)	Veggie Rice Paper Rolls (p. 38) made with tofu or shrimp (make extra for lunch tomorrow!)
Day 3	Baked Blueberry Oatmeal (p. 14) + greek/dairy-free yogurt + sunflower seed butter	Veggie Rice Paper Rolls (p. 38)	Miso Sweet Potato Soup (p. 60) + whole grain or gluten-free toast	Spinach Pesto Frittata (p. 33) + roasted Thyme & Sage Veggies (p.52)
Day 4	Golden Mylk Chia Seed Pudding (p. 10) + 1 cup cantaloupe or banana	Everything Bagel Pita Chips (p. 27) + a warm mug of Miso Sweet Potato Soup (p. 60)	Carrots and whole grain crackers w/ Edamame Hummus (p. 68)	Shaved Brussel sprout, Feta, & Farro Salad (p. 50) w/ Herbed Turkey Meatballs (p. 41)
Day 5	Baked Blueberry Oatmeal (p. 14) + greek/dairy-free yogurt + sunflower seed butter	Oat & Seed Bar (p. 24) + 1 cup cantaloupe or other fruit	Spinach Pesto Frittata (p. 33) + Whole Grain Toast	Baked Salmon Nuggets (p. 36) + Parsnip Fries (p. 54)

Please note this is an example meal plan. Nutrition requirements will vary based on individual needs. Contact info@mollypelletier.com if you'd like to discuss personalized nutrition recommendations.

FOR THE MORNING

(quick, simple breakfasts... or a breakfast-for-dinner moment)

WHOLE GRAIN FRENCH TOAST STICKS

Ingredients (~2 servings)

- 4 slices whole grain bread (or sourdough, or gluten-free)
- 3 eggs
- 1/4 cup almond milk or other milk
- 1/2 tsp vanilla extract
- 2 tsp maple syrup
- 1/2 teaspoon cinnamon

1. In a medium-sized mixing bowl, combine eggs, vanilla, milk, cinnamon, and maple syrup until well combined. Slice your bread into 3 long pieces as shown here. Dunk your bread strips in the egg mixture for ~2 seconds on each side.
2. Heat a nonstick pan to medium heat and spray with avocado oil. Toast up your bread until golden brown (~3-5 min on each side).
3. Plate and top with your favorite toppings! I added fresh fruit, greek yogurt for more protein, and a touch of whip cream because why not.

Feel free to double or triple this recipe for meal prep and store in the fridge (up to 1 week) or freezer (up to 5 months).

Prep-ahead!

SPINACH & FETA EGG WHITE BITES

Ingredients (~10-12 bites)

- 2 cups baby spinach
- 1/2 cup crumbled feta (or df cheese alternative)
- 2 cups liquid egg whites (I used a carton of liquid egg whites for ease of use, but you can also sub for 10 egg whites or 7 whole eggs)
- 1.5 cups cottage cheese (can sub for 1 cup dairy-free cheese alternative)
- 1/2 tsp sea salt
- 1/2 tsp ground black pepper

1. Combine egg whites (or whole eggs if using) + cottage cheese + salt + pepper in a blender and combine for ~20 seconds until well mixed.
2. In a greased muffin tin (or use liners), tear a small handful of baby spinach and fill each muffin tin. Now pour over your egg mixture. Crumble feta on top.
3. Bake at 375 for 35-40 minutes. Allow to cool fully and use a knife to remove the egg bites. Store in an airtight container for up to 5 days.

GOLDEN MYLK CHIA SEED PUDDING

Ingredients (1 serving)

- 1/4 cup chia seeds
- 1 cup unsweetened almond or other milk
- 1/2 cup greek yogurt or nondairy yogurt (add 1 scoop collagen or vanilla protein powder if using dairy-free yogurt)
- 1/8 tsp cinnamon
- 1/8 tsp turmeric powder
- 1 tsp maple syrup
- 1/16 tsp (or one drop) vanilla extract

Toppings: granola, coconut, nuts or seeds of choice

Prep-ahead!

1. Mix all ingredients together in a small jar or container.
2. Allow to sit for 5 minutes, then give it another stir to make sure all the chia seeds are well combined. Pop back in the fridge for at least 1 hour to gel or overnight.
3. When ready to eat, remove from the fridge and top with granola, coconut, and/or fruit. Enjoy for a quick breakfast or snack. Store in the fridge for up to 6 days.

Tip: If you don't enjoy the texture of chia seeds, you can also blend this recipe until smooth.

BLUEBERRY VANILLA CHIA SEED PUDDING

Ingredients (1 serving)

- 1/4 cup chia seeds
- 1 cup almond milk
- 1/2 cup greek yogurt or dairy-free yogurt alternative (add 1 scoop collagen or vanilla protein powder if using dairy-free)
- 1/3 cup frozen or fresh blueberries
- 1/16 tsp (or one drop) of vanilla extract
- dash of cinnamon
- 1 tsp maple syrup (optional)

1. Mix all ingredients together in a small jar or container.
2. Allow to sit for 5 minutes, then give it another stir to make sure all the chia seeds are well combined. Pop back in the fridge for at least 1 hour to gel or overnight.
3. When ready to eat, remove from the fridge and top with granola, nut butter, and/or fruit. Enjoy for a quick breakfast or snack.

Double or triple this recipe for meal prep. Store in the fridge for up to 6 days.

Prep-ahead!

SWEET POTATO EGG NESTS

Ingredients (4 egg nests)

- 1-2 medium sweet potatoes
- 4 eggs
- 1 tsp avocado oil

1. Grab your washed sweet potato and place in a spiralizer. Spiralize until you've obtained about 2 cups of sweet potato noodles.
2. Heat a nonstick pan, then add 1 tsp of avocado oil. Place spiralized sweet potato in an oiled skillet.
3. Cook for about 5 minutes on low heat, or until sweet potatoes are about 50% done (Keep on low heat; sweet potatoes can burn easily).
4. Separate the sweet potato into 4 little piles with a small hole in the center, just like a bird's nest. Crack an egg in each nest.
5. Cover the pan with a lid to allow the top of the egg to cook faster.
6. If you want your egg to cook faster, throw 1/2 tsp of water into the pan and then cover with the lid to help steam the nests (I did this, which is why the eggs look slightly poached on top).
7. When eggs are cooked to your liking, remove them carefully with a spatula. Top with desired seasonings and enjoy!

WHIPPED STRAWBERRY FAUX-GURT

Ingredients (2-3 servings)

- 1 package organic silken tofu, drained
- 1 1/2 cups fresh or defrosted strawberries (+ an additional 1 1/2 cups for the bottom of the glass/jar)
- 1/2 tsp vanilla extract
- 1 tbsp maple syrup
- Optional additions: 1 tbsp hemp hearts, 1/2 tbsp psyllium husk for added gut-healthy prebiotic fiber

1. Simply drain silken tofu and add to blender with all 1 1/2 cups fresh or defrosted strawberries, 1/2 tsp vanilla extract, and 1 tbsp maple syrup. Blend for 1 min on high to aerate the yogurt.
2. Add fresh or defrosted strawberries to glass or jars. Pour your faux-gurt over the berries. Refrigerate for about 20 min to set.
3. When ready to consume, remove from the fridge and top with nuts, seeds, or nut butter. Perfect for an easy breakfast prep or a vegan dessert. Store in the fridge for up to 5 days.

Prep-ahead!

Prep-ahead!

BAKED BLUEBERRY CHIA OATMEAL

Ingredients (2 servings)

- 1 1/2 cups oats
- 2 cups unsweetened almond milk or other milk
- 3 tbsp chia seeds
- 1/2 cup blueberries
- 1 ripe banana, mashed
- 1/4 tsp vanilla extract
- 1/4 tsp cinnamon
- 1/2 tsp baking powder
- 1 tbsp maple syrup (optional)

1. Preheat oven to 350 F.
2. In a medium-sized mixing bowl, mix all ingredients until well combined. Transfer to two small, oven-safe ramekins. Bake for ~20 min at 350. (If you do not have small ramekins, you can also use a small 8x4 oven-safe baking dish and bake for ~25 minutes or until cooked to your liking).
3. When oatmeal is cooked to your preference, remove from the oven and get to topping! I used greek yogurt, sunflower seed butter, seeds, and coconut.
Store in the fridge for up to 5 days.

EGG & TOAST CUPS

Ingredients (12 cups)

- 12 eggs
- 12 slices of whole grain bread (or sourdough, or GF bread of choice)

1. Preheat oven to 350 F. Cut parchment into small squares to line your muffin tin.
2. Using your hands, press a slice of bread firmly into each of the parchment lined muffin tins, forming a small cup for your egg. Bake bread for 5 minutes.
3. Remove bread cups from oven and crack an egg inside. You can also add veggies, cheese, or whatever you like! Bake for 13-15 minutes depending on how cooked you like your eggs.
4. Allow to cool before removing from muffin tin.

Store in the fridge for up to 5-6 days.

Prep-ahead!

Microwave for ~60-90 seconds to reheat.

FLUFFIEST 4-INGREDIENT OATMEAL PANCAKES

Ingredients
(yields ~3 servings)

- 1 cup oats
- 1 cup plain greek yogurt (can sub for a dairy-free greek yogurt)
- 3 eggs
- 1/4 tsp vanilla extract
- 1/3 cup blueberries (optional)

1. Combine oats, eggs, yogurt, and vanilla extract all ingredients in a blender or food processor until well combined (~30 seconds).
2. Add in blueberries if you wish and give the batter a quick mix with a spoon.
3. Heat a nonstick pan. Turn to medium heat and spray or grease with avocado oil. Pour ~1/4 cup of your batter to make 3-4" pancakes. In a large pan, you can make 3-4 pancakes at once. Watch for bubbles and flip!
4. Create your stack and top with your favorite toppings: berries, sunflower seed butter, maple syrup, etc.

These pancakes can be easily prepped ahead and frozen (store in the freezer for up to 3 months)! They reheat deliciously well in the microwave.

Prep-ahead!

CREAMY MUSHROOM TOASTS

Ingredients (1 serving)

- 2 slices whole grain, sourdough, or gluten-free toast
- 4 tbsp store bought hummus
- 2 tbsp tahini
- 1 tsp coconut aminos
- 1 cup fresh or frozen mushrooms
- sesame seeds
- 1/16 tsp fine grain sea salt

Add a fried or soft-boiled egg (or a slice of tofu) for extra protein and nutrients!

1. Add 1 cup of fresh or frozen sliced mushrooms (I used frozen from Whole Foods) to a heated nonstick pan. Sauté until cooked well. if you're using frozen, sauté until the water has evaporated.
2. While mushrooms are cooking, toast your bread. Once toasted, spread on 2 tbsp of storebought (or homemade) hummus onto each slice of toast.
3. In your pan with the mushrooms, add 2 tbsp tahini, 1 tsp coconut aminos, and 1/16 tsp fine-grain salt. Stir for ~20 seconds to warm the tahini, then spoon the creamy mushrooms onto your toast. If you'd like to add a fried or soft-boiled egg on top, that is also delicious!
4. Optional: Drizzle on a little extra tahini, and sprinkle with flaky salt, sesame seeds.

VANILLA TAHINI PROTEIN SMOOTHIE

Ingredients (1 serving)

- 1 cup greek yogurt (or sub for nondairy yogurt + 1 scoop collagen powder or vanilla protein powder)
- 1 tbsp hemp hearts
- 1 tbsp tahini
- 1 small banana
- Dash of cinnamon (optional)
- 1/3 cup unsweetened almond milk or any milk
- 1 tsp maple syrup (optional)

1. Blend until smooth. Top with granola for added crunch.

To avoid reflux when drinking smoothies: chew (yes, chew!) to stimulate digestion and avoid chugging all at ounce. Sip over 7-10 minutes.

Prep-ahead!

GUT HEALTH GREEN SMOOTHIE

Ingredients (1 serving)

- 1/2 frozen banana
- 1/2 cup greek yogurt or nondairy alternative (add vanilla protein powder if using nondairy yogurt)
- 1/3 cup frozen zucchini (peeled, chopped and frozen ahead)
- 1/3 cup raspberries
- 1/2 tbsp hemp hearts
- 1/2 tbsp chia seeds
- 1 tsp maple syrup or 1 date (optional, for sweetness)
- 1/2 cup unsweetened nut milk or dairy milk of choice

1. Combine ingredients in a blender and blend until well combined.
2. Top with hemp hearts.

To save time: prep ingredients in baggies and freeze for easy morning smoothies.

FROTHY TURMERIC LATTÉ

Ingredients (1 serving)

- 1 cup unsweetened almond or coconut milk
- 1/8 tsp turmeric powder or grated turmeric root
- 1 tsp maple syrup
- 1/8 tsp cinnamon
- 1/16 tsp vanilla extract
- 1 tbsp hemp hearts
- optional additions:
    - [1 scoop vanilla protein powder](#)
    - 1/8 tsp ginger powder (as tolerated, person-dependent)

1. Add all ingredients to a blender. Blend on high until frothy (~60 seconds).

2. Warm liquid on stove top on in a microwave safe mug in the microwave,

A warm, cozy caffeine-free beverage or coffee alternative.

SNACKS

APPLE WALNUT MUFFINS

Ingredients (~8 muffins)

- Dry:
  - 2 cups almond flour
  - 1/2 teaspoon baking soda
  - 1/8 teaspoon fine-grain sea salt
  - 1 teaspoon cinnamon
  - 1/4 cup crushed walnuts + 1/4 cup crushed walnuts for topping (optional)
- Wet:
  - 1 large apple grated and drained (+ 1/2 of another apple for decoration if desired)
  - 3 eggs, whiskey
  - 1/4 cup honey
  - 3 tbsp molasses
  - 1 tablespoon coconut oil, melted

1. Preheat oven to 325 degrees F and grease or line muffin tin.
2. Combine dry ingredients in large bowl. Drain grated apple in a cheese cloth or paper towel. Add all wet ingredients to dry and mix until combined.
3. Using a spoon or cookie scoop, fill muffin cups ~ 3/4 full.
4. Bake for 23-25 minutes, until golden brown and toothpick inserted in center comes out clean. Allow to cool fully. Store in the fridge for up to 1 week.

BANANA BREAD MUFFINS
with crunchy granola topping and vanilla glaze

Ingredients (10-12 muffins)

- 2 ripe bananas, mashed
- 1 1/4 cup of almond flour
- 2 tbsp arrowroot starch
- 3 eggs, whisked
- 1 tsp vanilla extract
- 1/2 teaspoon baking powder
- 1/4 cup coconut sugar
- 2 tsp cinnamon
- 1/8 tsp fine grain salt
- Optional toppings:
    - 1/3 cup granola
    - vanilla glaze: 2 tbsp protein powder + 1/4 cup powdered sugar + 2 tbsp water

Prep-ahead!

1. Preheat oven to 350 F.
2. In a mixing bowl, combine ingredients all wet ingredients (mashed bananas, whisked eggs, vanilla). Then slowly add in dry ingredients (almond flour, arrowroot starch, coconut sugar, baking powder, cinnamon, salt).
3. Fill a greased muffin tip 3/4 of the way with your batter. Sprinkle muffins with 1 tsp granola each. Bake for ~22-24 min. Allow them to cool fully.
4. Mix glaze ingredients in a small bowl. Once your muffins have cooled, drizzle on your glaze, Store in the fridge for up to 6 days.

OAT & SEED BARS

Ingredients (~6 bars)

- 1 1/4 cup oats
- 1 cup room temperature creamy sunflower seed butter
- 1/2 cup crushed walnuts
- 1/3 cup seeds of choice, or another type of crushed nut
- 2 tbsp flax meal
- 1/4 cup maple syrup or honey
- 1 tsp vanilla extract
- 1/8 tsp salt
- Optional toppings:
    - 1 /4 cup white chocolate chips, melted
    - hemp seeds
    - nuts

1. In a large mixing bowl, add all ingredients and mix until well combined.
2. Line a square baking dish with parchment paper and add your dough. Press down with your fingers until the dough forms a thick, even layer. Optional: top with nuts, white chocolate drizzle, chia, hemp seeds, whatever you like!
3. Freeze for about 45 minutes to set. When ready to eat, slice and enjoy. Store in the fridge or freezer.

Prep-ahead!

PUMPKIN "PERFECT" BARS

Ingredients (~4-5 bars)

- 1/2 cup creamy sunflower seed butter
- 1/4 cup vanilla protein powder
- 1/3 cup pumpkin puree
- 2 tbsp maple syrup
- 1 tsp pumpkin pie spice
- 1/2 tsp cinnamon
- Topping: 1/4 cup white chocolate chips, melted

Prep-ahead!

1. Combine all ingredients until you have a nice thick dough that sticks to itself but not to your hands. If your dough is too dry (could be due to your protein powder absorbing more water), add another tbsp of pumpkin puree or maple syrup. If the dough is too wet, add a touch more protein powder.
2. Line a small squash pan with parchment paper and press into the pan until you have a dense, flat, square shape. Optional: melt your chocolate chips in the microwave for 60-90 seconds, then drizzle on top using a spoon.
3. Freeze for 1 hour to set. Remove the freezer and allow to thaw for 5 minutes. Slice into 4 small bars.
4. Store in the fridge for up to 7 days or freezer for up to 6 months.

NUT & SEED GRANOLA

Ingredients (yields ~5 cups)

- 2 cups oats
- 1 cup mixed nuts of choice (pecans, walnuts)
- 1/2 cup sunflower or pumpkin seeds
- 2 tbsp coconut oil, melted
- 1/3 cup maple syrup
- 1/2 tsp vanilla extract
- 1/2 teaspoon cinnamon
- 1/8 tsp fine grain salt

1. Preheat the oven to 325 F. In a large mixing bowl, combine all ingredients. If you're using pecans/walnuts, be sure to crush or chop. Combine all ingredients until well-mixed.
2. On a parchment-covered baking sheet, spread your granola mixture out in a thin layer. Bake for 15 minutes, flip toss, then bake for another 10 minutes or until crispy and totally dry.
3. When the granola is crisp and golden brown, remove and allow to cool fully before breaking into chunks and transferring to an air-tight container.

Top this over yogurt, smoothies, milk, or just straight out of the jar as a snack with a piece of fruit.

Prep-ahead!

"EVERYTHING BAGEL" PITA CHIPS

Ingredients (~48 chips)

- 4 medium or large whole wheat pitas
- 2-3 tbsp garlic-infused olive oil
- 1/2 tsp garlic powder (optional)
- 1/4 tsp sea salt
- 1 tbsp sesame seeds
- 1 tbsp poppy seads

1. Preheat oven to 400 degrees. Use the convection roast setting if you have it.
2. Use kitchen shears or clean scissors to separate pita into sheets and cut into 6 small triangles.
3. Throw pita triangles in a big bowl. Toss with 2-3 tbsp of garlic-infused olive oil until all of the pieces are lightly coated.
4. Mix seasonings and seeds in a smaller bowl, and then toss over pita. Mix and coat the pita triangles until seasonings/seeds are evenly distributed.
5. Cover 2-3 baking sheets with parchment, and evenly distribute pita on your sheets so that they don't overlap or touch.
6. Bake for about 5-7 minutes. Flip. Bake for another 1-2 minutes until crunchy and toasted. Watch carefully as they can crisp up quickly.

You can also make cinnamon sugar or rosemary sea salt flavor pita chips by switching up the seasonings!

CARROT CAKE BITES

Ingredients (~8-10 bites)

- 1/2 cup grated carrot
- 1 cup oat flour
- 1/4 cup crushed pecans or walnuts
- 2 tbsp unsweetened shredded coconut (+ additional 3 tbsp for rolling the bites)
- 2 tbsp maple syrup
- 1/4 cup room temperature tahini
- 1 tsp cinnamon
- 1/16 tsp nutmeg (optional)
- 1 tsp vanilla extract
- 1/4 tsp salt

1. In a mixing bowl, combine oat flour, crushed walnuts or pecans, 2 tablespoons of shredded coconut, cinnamon, vanilla, cinnamon, salt, tahini & maple syrup. Mix until well combined.
2. Using your hands, mix in your grated carrots until well combined.
3. Place 3 tbsp of shredded coconut on a small plate. Roll carrot mixture into about 8-10 even balls. Roll each ball into coconut. Store in the fridge in an airtight container for up to 6 days.

Prep-ahead!

COCONUT YOGURT POPSICLES

Ingredients (~4 popsicles)

- 1 1/2 cups unsweetened coconut yogurt
- 1/2 cup frozen fruit of choice (I used mixed berries)
- 1 tsp vanilla extract
- 2 tbsp maple syrup
- 1/4 cup almond milk
- dash of fine grain salt

1. Simply blend all ingredients in a blender or food processor until well combined.
2. Taste to make sure it's sweet enough for you. If not, add more maple syrup. Pour mixture into pop molds (or if you don't have molds, use cups with tongue depressors or spoons). You could also get fancy here and add granola on the bottom for a yogurt/granola pop!
3. Freeze for at least 2-3 hours or until hardened. When ready to consume, run the molds under hot water for 20 seconds and twist the pops out.

NO-BAKE COCONUT GRANOLA CUPS

Ingredients (4 cups)

- 1/2 cup unsweetened shredded coconut
- 1/2 cup creamy sunflower seed butter
- 1/4 cup whole oats
- 1/4 cup oat flour
- 2 tbsp maple syrup
- 1/4 cup crushed walnuts
- 1 tsp cinnamon
- 1 tsp vanilla extract
- 1/8 tsp of fine grain salt

Prep-ahead!

1. Mix all ingredients well until you have a thick dough that sticks together, and not to your hands.
2. Line a muffin tin with 4 cupcake liners. Press 1/2 cup of the dough into each liner. Sprinkle with shredded coconut.
3. Pop the cups back in the freezer to set for at least 20 min. Store in the freezer for up to 6 months (but they won't last that long).

BAKED PUMPKIN MUFFIN DONUTS

Ingredients (~5-6 donuts)

- 1 1/4 cup almond flour
- 2 tbsp arrowroot starch
- 2 tbsp coconut sugar
- 1/3 cup pumpkin puree
- 2 eggs, whisked
- 1 tbsp coconut oil, melted
- 2 tbsp maple syrup
- 1 tsp baking powder
- 1 tsp vanilla extract
- 1 tsp pumpkin pie spice
- 1/8 tsp fine-grain salt
- Optional Icing:
    - 1/4 cup coconut butter + 1 tbsp maple syrup + 1/16 tsp pumpkin pie spice

1. Preheat oven to 350 F. In a large mixing bowl, combine eggs, pumpkin, coconut oil, and maple syrup. Then slowly add all dry ingredients (almond flour, baking powder, arrowroot starch, pumpkin pie spice, coconut sugar). Mix until combined.
2. Spray or grease a silicone mini donut mold with avocado oil or coconut oil. Distribute the mixture to the molds, filling the molds 3/4 of the way up. Bake for 22 min at 350.
3. Remove and allow to cool fully before removing from molds.
4. Mix your icing ingredients and add a dash of pumpkin pie spice for flavor. Drizzle on your icing.

SAVORY

(simple, savory recipes for lunch or dinner)

SPINACH PESTO FRITTATA

Ingredients (~4-5 servings)

- 12 eggs, whisked
- 1/3 cup milk or non-dairy milk
- 3 cups raw spinach or other leafy green
- 1/3 cup pesto (can use store bought or use my **Spinach Basil Pesto** if sensitive to garlic)
- 1/2 tsp salt
- 1 tbsp avocado oil
- optional: 1/3 cup goat cheese crumbled on top

1. Preheat the oven to 350. Pour 1 tbsp avocado oil into a medium sized cast iron skillet or baking dish. Use your hands to grease the pan or dish.
2. In a large mixing bowl, combine your eggs, milk, salt, and pesto. Whisk until fluffy.
3. Next, add chopped spinach and any other chopped veggies to skillet/dish. Now, pour egg mixture on top of your veggies. Optional: Sprinkle on salt, pepper, goat cheese, etc.
4. Bake for 30 minutes or until eggs are cooked to your liking.

Prep-ahead!

I love prepping this ahead for busy weeks to grab out of the fridge and quickly reheat. Paired with whole grain toast, this is an easy and delicious 5-minute meal.

Store in the fridge for up to 5-6 days.

CRISPY TEMPE & CARROT NOODLE STIR FRY

Ingredients (~4 servings)

- 10 large carrots
- 1, 8oz package of tempe
- 2 cups cauliflower florets
- 2 cups de-stemmed kale, chopped
- 2 eggs, whisked
- 4 tbsp coconut aminos
- 1 1/2 tbsp sesame oil or garlic-infused olive oil
- 1/4 tsp sesame seeds
- 1/4 tsp garlic powder (as tolerated)
- 1/8 tsp salt

1. Slice tempe into about 1 cm thick slices and place to the side. Begin peeling the carrots with a vegetable peeler, removing the skin first, and then creating long noodles. Place noodles to the side.

2. Heat a hot nonstick pan to medium-high heat then add 1 tbsp sesame or garlic oil. Add in tempe and allow to crisp until golden brown (Note: tempe is already fully cooked, we are just getting a golden crust on it here!). As tempe is cooking, add cauliflower and kale to the pan. Cook until veggies are tender (~7-9 min), then add carrot noodles. Saute until carrots are slightly cooked (~4-6 min).

3. Move tempe/veggies over to one side of the pan. Crack two eggs into the side of the pan, and begin scrambling. Keep the eggs moving!

4. After the egg is cooked (~5 min), begin to combine the eggs with the rest of the stir fry. Toss veggies, egg, and tempe until combined.

5. Add coconut aminos, 1/2 tbsp sesame or olive oil, sesame seeds, salt, and any other desired seasonings. Lightly toss.

6. Plate your stir fry and garnish with sesame seeds.

Prep-ahead!

5-MINUTE AVOCADO EGG SALAD

**Ingredients
(4-5 servings)**

- 6 eggs, hardboiled
- 1 large ripe avocado (can substitute for 1/2 cup hummus if you do not like avocado)
- salt and pepper as desired

1. Hard boil 6 eggs (boil for 10-12 min), then cool and peel (use a spoon for easy shell removal!)
2. Dice your eggs into small 1/2" pieces
3. Peel and mash 1 large, ripe avocado. Mix with diced egg. Add any seasonings, salt, pepper if you like. Keep mashing until well combined. (You can also add hummus if your avocado was too small or if you prefer hummus over avocado).
4. Now add your avocado egg salad to two slices of toasted bread with fresh greens. Sprinkle on hemp seeds for additional nutrition if you like!

CRISPY BAKED SALMON NUGGETS

Ingredients
(~3-4 servings / 15-17 nuggets)

- 1 lb salmon filet, skin removed (ask your fishmonger and he will probably do it for you!)
- 1 1/2 cups Italian bread crumbs (can use gluten-free breadcrumbs if desired)
- 3 tbsp avocado oil
- 2 tbsp honey
- 1 tsp salt
- 1 cup plain, greek yogurt (can substitute for unsweetened plain dairy-free yogurt)
- Juice of 1/2 lemon
- Spray avocado oil, or 1/2 tsp avocado oil

1. Preheat oven to 400 degrees F
2. Cut your salmon into small 1-1.5" nuggets
3. In a bowl, mix together breadcrumbs, honey, avocado oil, and 1/2 tsp salt.
4. In another bowl, mix together greek yogurt + 1/2 tsp salt + lemon juice
5. Time to get messy! Coat the salmon pieces in yogurt mix, then in your breadcrumb mixture.
6. Place salmon bites onto a parchment-covered baking sheet or a baking rack if you have one. If you have spray avocado oil, spray your nuggets with a light layer of oil (helps to crisp them) or use a brush to lightly coat the nuggets. Bake at 400F for 15 minutes.

Pair with rice and roasted veggies, or Parsnip Fries. Or toss on a salad/grain bowl for an easy lunch.

MEDITERRANEAN CHICKEN STUFFED PEPPERS

Ingredients (~4 servings)

- 1 lb ground chicken
- 4 bell peppers
- 1 small zucchini, finely chopped
- 1 cup cooked white or brown rice
- 1 avocado, diced
- 1/2 tsp salt, 1 tsp Za'atar seasoning
- Shredded cheese of choice (can use dairy-free)

1. Slice in half and de-seed your bell peppers. Place open side up and roast for 10 min at 375 degrees F.
2. While these are roasted, sauté ground chicken. When chicken is halfway cooked, add chopped zucchini and continue to sauté. Cook until chicken is no longer pink and/or greater than 165 F. Once cooked, stir in seasonings and cooked rice. Mix well.
3. Remove the peppers from the oven and fill with meat/rice mixture! Sprinkle with cheese and bake for 5 minutes at 400.
4. Once the cheese has melted, remove from the oven and top with sliced avocado and a sprinkle of sea salt.

Prep-ahead!

Depending on the size of your peppers, you may have leftover filling. Enjoy this on the side or add to a breakfast burrito.

VEGGIE RICE PAPER ROLLS

Ingredients (~12 rolls)

- 12 ounces protein of choice: tempe, tofu, salmon, or shrimp
- 12 round rice paper wraps (I usually find these near the nori and sushi rice)
- 1 large avocado
- 6-8 leaves of romaine
- 1 red bell pepper
- 5 small seedless cucumbers
- 1/4 cup sesame seeds

Dip these in my Sesame "Peanut" Sauce!

Prep-ahead!

1. Cook desired protein and slice into small, 1 oz slivers. Set aside.
2. Slice all veggies into small slivers as shown above and set aside.
3. Open your package of rice paper wrappers. Grab a large plate or baking dish and fill it with 1" of water (enough to submerge your wrappers). With clean hands, submerge the rice paper wrapper for ~10 seconds or you can feel the wrapper become slightly soft.
4. On a clean cutting board, place your wrapper and fill with 1 oz protein, small slice of avocado, cucumber, romaine, and bell pepper. Roll and tuck in the edges. Don't worry if they aren't perfect: rolling can take a little practice. They will still be delicious no matter how they look.
5. Sprinkle your rice paper rolls with sesame seeds and sea salt (optional). Dip in my Sesame "Peanut" Sauce or a pre-made peanut sauce.

Tips for folding:

Avoid over-filling. If your wraps are falling apart, submerge in water for less time. If your wraps are still crunchy, submerge in water for an additional few seconds before filling.

SESAME CUCUMBER SALAD

Ingredients (~4-5 servings)

- 2 medium-sized **seedless** cucumbers, or 6-7 Persian cucumbers, diced into 1" pieces
- 1 tbsp sesame oil
- 1 tbsp honey (or maple syrup)
- 2 tbsp coconut aminos
- 1 tablespoon sesame seeds

1. Wash and dry cucumbers. Dice into 1" pieces.
2. In a small bowl, mix sesame oil, honey, soy sauce, and sesame seeds.
3. In a medium-sized mixing bowl, combine cucumbers and sesame sauce until cucumbers are coated evenly.

Pair with white rice, tuna/salmon/or tofu, diced mango, and toasted seaweed for an easy "poke" bowl.

HERBED TURKEY MEATBALLS

Ingredients (~20 meatballs/4 servings)

- 1 lb lean ground turkey
- 1/3 cup breadcrumbs or gluten free oats
- 1/3 cup finely chopped fresh herbs (such as basil and/or parsley)
- 1/2 teaspoon dried oregano
- 1/3 cup grated Parmesan cheese (optional)
- 1 tsp fine grain salt
- 2 large eggs, whisked
- spray avocado oil or 1 tsp avocado oil

1. Preheat oven to 375 degrees F. If you are using oats instead of breadcrumbs, grind them in a blender or food processor.
2. In a large mixing bowl, combine breadcrumbs or your blended oats, chopped herbs, dried oregano, cheese (optional), and salt. Then, add in your turkey and whisked egg. Combine with your hands until just well combined (don't over mix).
3. Using a spoon or cookie scoop, create 1 1/2 inch balls and place on a parchment covered baking sheet (~20 balls).
4. Lightly brush (or spray) the meatballs with avocado oil. Bake for 18 minutes or until 165 F internal temperature. Store in an airtight container in the fridge for up to 5 days or in the freezer for up to 2 months.

Prep-ahead!

Top over a <u>farro salad</u>, or add to a piece of pita bread with roasted veggies. Delicious with tzatziki and hummus.

Prep-ahead!

LENTIL WRAPS

Ingredients (~15, 6" wraps)

- 1 cup dried red lentils
- 2 cups filtered water
- 1/2 tsp salt
- optional seasonings: 1/4 tsp dried basil, 1/4 tsp dried oregano
- Spray avocado oil or 1 tsp avocado oil

- If you want to make sweet lentil crêpes: substitute salt for 1 tbsp coconut sugar and 1/2 tsp cinnamon

1. In a medium-sized bowl, rinse and drain lentils 2-3 times.
2. In the same bowl, add 2 cups filtered water to the lentils and allow to sit for ~4 hours on the counter.
3. After 4 hours has passed, add your lentils and the water to a blender with salt and desired seasonings. Blend for ~30-45 seconds until you have a thick, paste-like substance.
4. Heat a nonstick pan to medium heat, then spray/grease with avocado oil. Add 1/4 cup of your batter into the pan and spread as thin as you can (~1/2 cm thin). Watch for bubbles (~4-5 min) and flip. Continue until all your batter is used.
5. Store in an airtight container for up to 6 days.

<u>Topping ideas:</u>

Savory - soft scrambled eggs + fresh herbs, avocado + grilled chicken, tzakiki + <u>Herbed Turkey Meatballs</u>

Sweet - ricotta + stewed strawberries, figs + greek yogurt + honey, or whipped cream + pistachios.

SCALLOPS TWO WAYS

Simple Seared Scallops
Ingredients (~4 servings)

- 1 lb scallops
- 1-2 tbsp avocado oil
- 1/8 tsp salt
- 1/8 tsp black pepper (optional)

1. Start by removing the small side muscle from the scallops. Then thoroughly pat your scallops dry with a paper towel. Sprinkle with salt and optional pepper.
2. Heat a 12-14" skillet (cast iron or nonstick), to high heat. Then add 1-2 tbsp avocado oil. Once oil begins to bubble, gently add your scallops, making sure they are not touching each other.
3. Sear the scallops for exactly 2 minutes on each side. The scallops should have a light golden crust on each side. Serve immediately.

Simple Seared Scallops

Parmesan Breadcrumb Scallops

Parmesan Breadcrumb Scallops
Ingredients (~4 servings)

- 1 lb scallops
- 1 tbsp avocado oil
- 1/2 cup Italian breadcrumbs (can substitute for gluten-free breadcrumbs)
- 1/4 cup parmesan cheese
- 1/8 tsp salt
- 1/8 tsp black pepper (optional)

1. Start by removing the small side muscle from the scallops. Then thoroughly pat your scallops dry with a paper towel.
2. Combine avocado oil, breadcrumbs, parmesan, salt, and pepper in a small bowl.
3. Place your scallops in an 8x10 baking dish. Pour the breadcrumb mixture on top.
4. Bake for 15-18 min or until internal temperature is 145 F.

Pair with roasted potatoes and <u>carrots</u> for a cozy weeknight meal.

SHEET PAN ZA'ATAR SALMON
with garlicky roasted vegetables

Ingredients
(2 servings)

- two 4-6 oz salmon fillets
- 1 cup broccoli
- 2 large carrots
- 1 large white or sweet potato (or 2 small-medium potatoes)
- 2 tbsp garlic-infused olve oil
- 1/8 tsp salt
- 1/4 tsp za'atar seasoning

1. Preheat your oven to 375 degrees F. Wash and dry your carrots, broccoli, and potatoes. Chop broccoli and slice all carrots/potatoes into small 1/2" pieces.
2. Toss your veggies in 2 tbsp garlic-infused olive oil and 1/8 tsp salt. Spread your veggies out on a parchment-covered baking sheet. Place salmon fillets in the center. Sprinkle salmon with 1/4 tsp za'atar seasoning.
3. Pop your salmon and veggies into the oven. Bake for ~15- minutes. Check that your salmon is cooked (thickest part 145 F degrees or appears flaky/light pink). If you prefer your veggies more cooked, remove salmon and pop the veggies back in.

4. Once veggies are cooked to your liking, remove from the oven and plate.
Optional: Drizzle veggies with **Pesto** or **Tahini Herb Dressing**.

Feel free to substitute salmon here for chicken, tofu, or tempe.

SALMON RICE BOWL
with maple "soy" marinade

Ingredients (2 servings)

- two 4-6 oz salmon fillets
- 2 tbsp coconut aminos
- 1/2 tsp sesame oil
- 1 tsp maple syrup
- 3 large carrots, shredded
- 2 mini persian cucumbers, thinly sliced
- 1 tsp sesame seeds
- 1 cup cooked brown or white rice

1. Preheat your oven to 375 degrees F. In a small bowl, combine 2 tbsp coconut aminos, 1/2 tsp sesame oil, and 1 tsp maple syrup. Place your salmon (flesh side down) into the marinade while the oven preheats.
2. Shred carrots and slice cucumber. Set aside.
3. Place your salmon on a parchment-lined baking sheet and bake for ~10-11 minutes or until cooked as desired (thickest part 145 F degrees).
4. In a bowl, add 1/2 cup rice, 1/2 cup grated carrot, and 1/2 of your diced cucumber.
5. Once your salmon is cooked, remove it from the oven and dice into ~1" pieces. Add to your bowl. Sprinkle with sesame seeds. Optional: add a drizzle of coconut aminos.

SHRIMP TACO NIGHT
with mango avocado salsa

Ingredients (~4 servings)

- 8-10 small tortillas (organic flour, corn, or Siete grain-free)
- 1 lb shrimp (fresh or frozen)
- 2 large zucchini, diced into 1" pieces
- 2 cups cooked white or brown rice
- 1 can vegetarian (lard-free) refried black beans
- Ingredients for salsa:
    - 1 avocado, diced into 1 cm pieces
    - 1 mango, diced into 1 cm pieces
    - 1 small cucumber, diced into 1 cm pieces
    - 1/3 cup finely chopped cilantro
    - juice of 1/2 lime
- Flavors & seasonings:
    - 2 tbsp garlic-infused olive oil
    - 1/2 tsp salt, 1 tsp Za'atar
- Toppings:
    - shredded lettuce, sesame seeds, toasted nuts or seeds, shredded cheese (optional)

Tips:

- **You can substitute shrimp here with crumbled tempe, tofu, or ground turkey.**

- **To save time, skip the sauteed zucchini taco filling and go with a bagged shredded cabbage mix.**

SHRIMP TACO NIGHT
with mango avocado salsa

1. Start by combining diced mango, diced cucumber, diced avocado, finely chopped cilantro, and juice of 1/2 lime for your salsa. Set aside.
2. Gather additional toppings you may want for your tacos such as toasted nuts/seeds, shredded lettuce, and cheese. Add to small bowls and set aside.
3. Now heat two large nonstick pans, then add 1 tbsp garlic-infused olive oil in each. In one pan, add your defrosted or fresh shrimp (tails removed). In the other pan, add your diced zucchini. Saute until zucchini is slightly soft (~8-10 min), then toss with za'atar seasoning. Cook shrimp until totally white and fully cooked (165 F internal temperature). Note: If you prefer to save time, you can skip the zucchini and opt for a bagged shredded cabbage mix for the veggie filling.

4. In a pot or pan, warm your vegetarian refried black beans until hot. Sprinkle with sesame seeds and/or flaky sea salt. Add to a small bowl for serving.

5. Warm your tortillas; either over an open flame on the stovetop or in the oven wrapped in tin foil (I prefer the latter option). Also, warm your cooked rice here if you have not freshly prepared it as directed on the container. You can also use your oven here at 200 F to keep all ingredients warm until serving.

6. When you are ready to serve, add all ingredients to bowls and place on the table. Time to build your taco - Use your tortilla as a base, add a little bit of zucchini, rice, shrimp, 1-2 tbsp mango salsa, crunchy nuts, and/or cheese.

CRISPY KALE CHICKEN QUESADILLAS

Best way to eat a salad's-worth of kale, without even picking up a fork! You can easily pack these quesadillas for a handheld lunch, or dip in guacamole for a satisfying dinner.

Ingredients (~4 small quesadillas)

- 8 small tortillas (organic corn, flour, or Siete grain-free tortillas)
- 12 oz shredded chicken (~2 chicken breasts)
- 1 cup shredded cheddar cheese (can sub for dairy-free)
- 1/2 cup crumbled cotija cheese (can sub for dairy-free feta)
- 5-6 cups raw kale
- 2 tbsp avocado oil

1. Preheat oven to 375 F. Place chicken breasts on a parchment-covered baking sheet and roast for 25-30 min or until cooked (165 F internal temp). Once cooked, remove and allow to cool until you can safely shred with a fork. Set aside.
2. Wash and de-stem kale. Dry completely with a dish towel or paper towels, then toss in 1 tbsp avocado oil until leaves are lightly coated. Spread your leaves out in one layer with ample space (leaves not touching) on a parchment-covered baking sheet. Pop in the oven and roast for 5-7 min. Flip, then roast for 2-4 more minutes until light and crisp. Remove from the oven and set aside.
3. Heat a medium-sized nonstick pan or skillet. Once hot, add 1 tbsp avocado oil. You will know the pan is hot enough when the oil is glistening. Then add one tortilla and top with 1/4 cup cheddar cheese, a large handful of crispy kale, and ~3 oz shredded chicken. Top with another tortilla (or you can fold it in half as shown above).
4. After the cheese has melted and the bottom tortilla is crispy, use a large spatula to carefully flip to sear both sides. Remove once the cheese is gooey and both the top and bottom tortillas are crisp. Top with cotija cheese and slice into triangles.

BLACK BEAN & QUINOA STUFFED SWEET POTATO

Ingredients
(yields~2 stuffed sweet potatoes)

- 2 small or medium sweet potatoes
- 3/4 cup canned black beans, drained and dried
- 1 cup cooked quinoa (or 1/4 cup dried quinoa)
- 1/2 medium avocado, diced
- 1/2 tsp za'atar seasoning
- 1/2 tsp garlic powder (optional)
- 1 tbsp extra virgin olive oil or garlic-infused oil
- juice of 1/2 lime
- 1/8 tsp fine-grain salt

1. Preheat oven to 400 F. Wash and dry sweet potatoes and place on a parchment-covered baking sheet. Pierce the sweet potatoes 2-3 times with a fork. Roast for 30-35 min or until soft.
2. While your sweet potatoes are baking, cook quinoa as directed on the package (1:2 cups quinoa to cups water ratio). Once cooked, mix quinoa with drained and rinsed black beans in a medium mixing bowl. Add extra virgin olive oil, za'atar, garlic powder, juice of 1/2 lime, and salt.
3. Once your sweet potatoes are cooked/soft, remove them from the oven and allow to cool until they can be safely handled. Once cooled, slice them open and create a little opening for your quinoa/black bean mixture.
4. Stuff your sweet potatoes with your quinoa/ black bean mixture. Then top with diced avocado and a pinch of sea salt.

Prep-ahead!

Pair with an additional protein source such as baked tofu or hummus and roasted broccoli for a complete meal.

SHAVED BRUSSEL SPROUT, FETA, & FARRO SALAD

Ingredients (yields ~10 cups)

- 4 cups shredded brussel sprouts (can buy pre-shredded or shred yourself)
- 1 1/2 cups dried farro
- 1 cup crumbled feta (can substitute dairy-free feta)
- 1/2 cup pumpkin seeds
- 1 tsp extra virgin olive oil
- 1/3 cup chopped fresh parsley (or other fresh herb)
- 1/4 tsp salt
- 1 tbsp avocado oil
- 1-2 tbsp extra virgin olive oil
- juice of 1/2 lemon (optional, as tolerated)

Top with roasted chicken, salmon, or tempe for an easy weeknight meal.

1. Preheat the oven to 375 F. If your brussel sprouts are whole, use a mandolin or food processor to shred them. Toss your shredded brussel sprouts in 1-2 tbsp avocado oil and 1/8 tsp salt. Spread shredded brussels on a parchment-covered baking sheet and roast for about 15 minutes or until golden brown and crispy.
2. Add dried farro to a pot with 3 cups water (2:1 ratio of water to cups of farro). Bring water to a boil. Then cover and simmer over low heat for about 25 minutes, or until the farro is tender and water is fully absorbed.
3. When finished cooking, allow both the farro and roasted brussel sprouts to cool to room temp. Once cooled, toss brussels and farro with feta, chopped parsley, 1 tsp extra virgin olive oil, and pumpkin seeds. Add salt and lemon juice to taste.
4. Pop in the fridge to serve chilled or eat straight away. When ready to serve, top with more feta, finely chopped parsley, and pepitas.

SESAME "PEANUT" NOODLES
with edamame and shaved carrot

Ingredients (~4 servings)

- 1, 8oz soba noodles (can substitute for rice noodles)
- 1 cup Sesame "Peanut" Sauce
- 1 1/2 cups edamame beans
- 2 large carrots
- 1 cup baby spinach
- 1/2 cup toasted cashews
- 1 tsp avocado or sesame oil
- 1 tbsp sesame seeds (optional)

1. Cook soba noodles as directed on the package.
2. While these are cooking, wash and dry carrots. Using a vegetable peeler, create long carrot noodles by running the peeler along the carrot. Continue until all carrots have been transformed into noodles.
3. If your edamame is frozen, defrost in the microwave, drain, and set aside.
4. Heat a large skillet to medium heat. Once your noodles are almost cooked, drain and add to a skillet with 1 tsp avocado or sesame oil. Add your carrot noodles and cook for ~2-5 minutes. Add spinach, edamame, and Sesame "Peanut" Sauce. Mix until all ingredients are warm.
5. When ready to serve, top with toasted cashews and/or sesame seeds.

Prep-ahead!

THYME & SAGE ROASTED ROOT VEGGIES

Ingredients (yields ~7-8 cups)

- 3 parsnips, diced into 1" pieces
- 2 medium sweet potatoes, diced into 1" pieces
- 1 small acorn squash, diced into 1" pieces
- 1-2 tbsp avocado oil
- 2 tsp dried thyme
- 1 tsp dried sage
- 1/4 tsp fine grain salt

1. Preheat oven to 375 F.
2. Wash and chop your root veggies into 1" pieces. In a large mixing bowl, combine veggies with avocado oil, dried thyme, dried sage, and salt.
3. Spread root veggies out on a parchment-covered baking sheet. Roast for ~22 minutes, flip and toss, and then roast for another ~10-12 minutes or until soft and tender.

These are the perfect meal prep for a lunch or dinner side dish. Pair with salmon, baked tofu, or roasted chicken.

WATERMELON BASIL FETA SALAD

Ingredients (yields ~ 10-12 cups)

- 1/2 large watermelon, diced (~8 cups)
- 1 large seedless cucumber, diced
- 1 cup crumbled feta (can sub for dairy-free feta)
- 12 basil leaves, finely chopped
- Juice of one lime (optional, as tolerated)
- 1/8 tsp fine-grain salt

1. Simply dice your watermelon and seedless cucumber into 1" pieces. Finely chop your basil.
2. Mix all ingredients with feta, lime juice, and fine-grain salt. It's that easy!

You can substitute watermelon for ANY melon such as cantaloupe or honeydew.

OVEN-BAKED PARSNIP FRIES

Ingredients (4-5 servings)

- 8-10 large parsnips
- 1-2 tbsp avocado oil
- 1/4 tsp salt
- 1/2 tsp za'atar seasoning

1. Preheat oven to 375 degrees F (on convection roast if you have that setting: best for getting veggies nice and crisp!)
2. Wash and dry parsnips. Peel if it's an older parsnip (tougher skin) or if you don't like the skin, but I like to keep the skin on. Slice parsnip into about 1/2" thick fry shapes.
3. In a large mixing bowl, toss parsnip fries in avocado oil, salt, and za'atar seasoning. Add any additional seasonings of choice (you could also make these sweet with cinnamon and coconut sugar).
4. Roast at 375 F for about 15 min. Flip and roast for another 10-15 min or until golden and crispy!
5. Dip in your favorite dip (see dip & sauce section).

Tip: Roast or saute with avocado oil as it has a higher smoke point and will not become rancid under high heat (up to 520 F).

SESAME ALMOND GREEN BEANS

Ingredients (yields ~8 cups)

- 2 lbs green beans
- 1/3 cup tahini
- 1/4 cup coconut aminos
- 1 tbsp sesame oil
- 1/2 cup shaved almonds
- 1/8 tsp flaky sea salt

1. Heat a large skillet or nonstick pan. Add your green beans and 1/4 cup water. Place the lid on the pan to allow them to lightly steam.
2. In a small bowl, combine tahini, coconut aminos, and sesame oil.
3. Once your green beans are cooked to your liking, drain and add to a serving dish.
4. Pour your sesame sauce over the green beans and toss. Then top with shaved almonds and flaky sea salt.

ROASTED RAINBOW CARROTS

with herbs & crumbled feta

Ingredients
(yields ~ 4 servings)

- 10-12 large tricolored carrots peeled and cut into 2" pieces
- 3/4 cup crumbled feta (can substitute for dairy-free feta)
- 1-2 tbsp avocado oil
- 1/8 tsp salt
- 1/4 tsp garlic powder (optional, as tolerated)
- 1 tsp dried thyme
- 1/2 tsp dried rosemary
- 2 tbsp finely chopped dill (optional)

1. Preheat the oven to 375 degrees F. Line a baking sheet with parchment paper. In a mixing bowl, toss chopped carrots with avocado oil, garlic powder, dried thyme, dried sage, and salt.
2. Once the vegetables are evenly coated, spread them out into a single layer on the parchment-covered baking sheet and place into the oven. Roast the carrots for ~20-25 min, taking them out at the halfway point to stir/flip.
3. Once the carrots are soft and slightly crisp on the outside, remove them and plate on a serving dish. Top with crumbled feta, fresh dill or a little bit more dried thyme, and a touch of salt.

ROSEMARY OLIVE OIL CROUTONS

Ingredients (~5-6 cups)

- 5-6 slices whole grain or sourdough bread (can use gluten-free)
- 1 tbsp avocado oil
- 1 tsp dried rosemary
- 1 tsp dried thyme
- 1/2 tsp fine grain sea salt

1. Preheat the oven to 325 degrees F.
2. Dice 5-6 slices of bread into approx. 1" squares.
3. Toss the bread cubes with 1 tbsp avocado oil until lightly coated. Then mix in your dried seasonings and salt. Toss until well coated.
4. Distribute the bread pieces on a parchment-lined baking sheet so they are not touching. Bake for 15-20 minutes, flipping/tossing occasionally, and watching to ensure they do not burn.
5. Remove when golden brown. Store in an airtight container in the pantry.

A delicious, easy way to upgrade any soup or salad.

SOUPS & SAUCES

Prep-ahead!

ANTI-INFLAMMATORY ROASTED VEGGIE SOUP

Ingredients (yield ~7-8 cups)

- 2 small sweet potatoes
- 1 cup chopped cauliflower florets
- 1 celery stalk
- 2 large carrots
- 1/2 cup pumpkin purée
- 3 cups chicken broth
- 1/2 cup canned coconut milk
- 1/2 tbsp turmeric powder
- 1/4 tsp ginger powder (as tolerated)
- juice of 1/2 lemon
- 1 tsp dried thyme
- 1/4 tsp salt
- 1/4 tsp black pepper
- 1 tbsp avocado oil

1. Preheat oven to 375 F. Roast chopped sweet potato, chopped celery, carrot, and cauliflower with 1 tbsp avocado oil until soft (~30 min).
2. When veggies are fork tender, remove and allow to cool. Add veggies to a blender with all other ingredients.
3. Blend on high until smooth and creamy. Season to taste. Add more broth or unsweetened nut milk if you'd like a thinner consistency.
4. Store in a sealed container in the fridge for up to 5-6 days. Top with your baked tofu, kale chips, or toasted pumpkin seeds.

MISO SWEET POTATO SOUP

Ingredients (~4 servings)

- 2 medium sweet potatoes, chopped
- 3 large carrots, diced
- 2 diced celery sticks, diced
- 6oz firm tofu (1/2 of a 12oz package)
- 3-4 cups chicken or veggie broth
- Juice of 1/2 lemon
- 1 tbsp white miso paste
- 3 tbsp nutritional yeast
- 2 tsp garlic-infused olive oil
- 1/2 tsp salt
- 1/4 tsp black pepper
- Optional: 3 scoops unflavored collagen powder for extra protein

1. Preheat the oven to 375 F. Toss diced sweet potato, carrots, and celery in 2 tbsp avocado oil and lay on a parchment-covered baking sheet. Roast for 20-25 minutes or until veggies are fork-tender.
2. Remove veggies from the oven and add to your blender with all other ingredients. Pulse a few times, then blend until smooth and creamy. Taste to make sure you love it! Add any additional seasonings you want.

I recommend topping with flaky salt, pumpkin seeds, and warm, toasty bread.

Prep-ahead!

WHITE BEAN SQUASH SOUP

Ingredients (yields 10-12 cups)

- 4 cups diced squash of choice (i.e. kabocha, butternut, etc)
- 2-4 medium sweet potatos potatoes
- 4 cups cooked or canned butter beans or white navy beans
- 2 celery stalks
- 2 large carrots
- 4 cups of chicken or veggie broth
- 1-2 tbsp avocado oil
- 1/2 tsp salt
- 1/2 tsp black pepper
- 1 tsp dried thyme (or fresh)
- 1 tsp dried sage
- 1 glove garlic or 1 tsp garlic powder (optional, as tolerated)
- juice of 1/2 lemon

1. Preheat oven to 350 F. Dice the squash into 1" pieces (note: If its a large squash, you may need to roast it whole for ~15 min and allow to cool in order to soften/slice). Cut squash, sweet potatoes, celery, and carrots into 1-2" cubes. Toss in 1-2 tbsp avocado oil and roast on a parchment-covered sheet pan at 350 until soft.
2. Once veggies are cooked, remove and allow to cool. Peel the skin off of your squash.
3. Now, in a large soup pot, add cooked squash and veggies with 3-4 cups of vegetable or chicken broth. Add in thyme, sage, and/or garlic clove if desired.
4. Bring to a boil, then down to a simmer. Allow to simmer on low heat until veggies are soft and basically falling apart.
5. Blend veggies + broth with a hand blender or allow to cool until you can safely add to a regular blender. Blend until smooth. Add 1-2 cups of broth if needed to blend.
6. Taste and add additional seasoning as needed. Top with a swirl of yogurt, nuts, seeds, and (of course) warm bread.

Prep-ahead!

CASHEW ALFREDO SAUCE

Ingredients (4-5 servings)

- 1 cup raw cashews (soaked in hot water for 30 minutes, or in cool water overnight)
- 1/3 cup nutritional yeast
- juice of 1/2 lemon
- 6oz silken tofu (1/2 of a 12oz package)
- 1/3 tsp salt (more if desired)
- 1/3 cup water (more if you need it to blend or if you like a thinner texture)

1. After soaking raw cashews in hot water (30 min) or in cool water (overnight), drain and rinse.
2. Simply combine all ingredients in a high-speed blender or food processor until well combined and creamy. It's that easy! Taste and make sure you like it. You could also add pesto or Italian seasoning depending on the color or flavor you're going for. If you want a thinner texture, add a little more water.
3. Warm in a pot or microwave, then pour over your favorite pasta. I used Explore Cuisine Black Bean pasta here.

Prep-ahead!

SPINACH BASIL PESTO

Ingredients (~16 tablespoons)

- 1/2 cup finely chopped fresh basil leaves
- 4 cups raw baby spinach
- 1/3 cup extra virgin olive oil (can also use garlic-infused olive oil)
- 1/2 cup pine nuts
- 1/4 cup grated parmesan (can substitute nutritional yeast if dairy-free)
- 1 tsp lemon juice (optional, as tolerated)
- 1/8 tsp salt (to taste)

1. Add all of your ingredients to a blender or food processor and process until you get your desired, pesto consistency.
2. Taste. Add additional salt if desired.

Use this pesto to top pasta and artichokes (as seen to the right), spread on sandwiches, cook eggs, or use as a salad dressing.

Prep-ahead!

HIGH PROTEIN BUTTERNUT SQUASH PASTA

Ingredients (~2 servings)

- 6 cups butternut squash, diced (~1 small butternut squash)
- 1 tbsp avocado oil
- 6 oz firm tofu (~1/2 12oz package)
- 1/3 cup nutritional yeast
- 1 tsp dried thyme
- 1/2 tsp dried sage
- 1/8 tsp cinnamon
- 1/2 tsp salt
- 1/8 tsp black pepper (as tolerated)
- juice of 1/2 lemon
- 1.5 cups unsweetened nut milk

1. Preheat oven to 375 F. Dice butternut squash into 1-2" pieces and remove all seeds (if you cannot cut the squash, roast for ~25 min first to soften before cutting). Toss diced butternut squash in 1 tbsp avocado oil. Roast diced butternut squash on a parchment-covered baking sheet until fork tender (~35 min).
2. When soft, remove the squash and allow it to cool until you can safely remove the skin without burning your hands. Remove the skin and add squash to a blender with all additional ingredients listed above.
3. Blend until smooth and creamy. If you would like a thinner sauce, add more nut milk. Taste and add additional seasonings if desired.

Pour over pasta and top with flaky sea salt. Warm toasted breadcrumbs are also delicious here!

SESAME "PEANUT" SAUCE

Ingredients (4 servings)

- 1/2 cup creamy sunflower seed butter
- 1 tsp sesame oil
- 1/4 cup coconut aminos
- 1 tbsp sesame seeds
- juice of 1/2 a lime
- 1/16 tsp salt

1. Simply combine all ingredients in a small mixing bowl. Store in the fridge for up to 7 days. Mix will before serving.

This sauce is delicious both warm or chilled on noodles and veggies. This can also be used as a dipping sauce for my <u>Veggie Rice Paper Rolls</u>.

PUMPKIN CREAM SAUCE

Ingredients (6-7 servings)

- 1 cup raw cashews (soaked in hot water for 30 minutes, or in cool water overnight)
- 3/4 cup pumpkin puree
- 1/2 cup water
- 1 tbsp garlic-infused olive oil
- 1/4 cup nutritional yeast
- 1/2 tsp fine-grain salt
- 1/2 tsp dried sage
- 1/2 tsp dried rosemary
- 1/4 tsp cracked black pepper (as tolerated)

1. Drain soaked cashews. Blend with all other ingredients in a high-speed blender for at least 30-40 seconds or until creamy.
2. Taste - feel free to add additional salt or any other seasonings here.
3. Warm your sauce on the stovetop or in the microwave.

Pour your creamy sauce on top of veggies, pasta, or use as a base for a delicious pumpkin cream soup.

DIPS & DRESSINGS

SILKY SMOOTH EDAMAME HUMMUS

Ingredients (yields ~2 cups)

- 1, 12oz package of frozen or fresh shelled edamame
- 1 1/2 tsp baking soda
- 4 tbsp garlic-infused olive oil
- 1/2 tsp pink salt
- 2 tbsp nutritional yeast
- juice of 1/2 a lemon
- Optional: 3-4 fresh basil leaves

1. Add edamame to boiling water with your baking soda to boil on medium heat and soften for about 10-12 minutes (8-9 minutes if using fresh). Remove the foam that rises to the top with a spoon as they cook. This process is what creates silky smooth hummus!
2. Once the beans are fork-tender, drain and add to your high-speed blender.
3. Add all other ingredients. Blend until smooth. taste to make sure you love it. Add more salt if needed.

Prep-ahead!

CARROT HUMMUS

Ingredients (yield ~2 cups)

- 1 lb carrots, diced into 1" pieces
- 1 cup canned chickpeas, drained and rinsed
- 1/4 cup tahini
- 1 tsp garlic-infused olive oil (+ 1 tsp for optional topping)
- 1 tbsp nutritional yeast
- 1/2 tsp salt
- optional: flaky sea salt or za'atar for topping

1. Add diced carrots to a microwave-safe bowl with enough water to cover them. Microwave carrots for 8-10 min until they are fork-tender (you can also boil them if you wish).
2. Drain carrots well and add them to a food processor or high-speed blender with all other ingredients. Blend until smooth or desired consistency is reached.
3. Pour your hummus into a bowl and top with flaky sea salt and a drizzle of garlic-infused olive oil (optional). Plate up with your fav veggies and crackers.

HERB TAHINI DRESSING

Ingredients (yield ~4 servings)

- 1/2 cup tahini
- 2 tbsp coconut aminos
- 1 tbsp water
- 1/2 tsp dried thyme
- 1/2 tsp dried rosemary
- 1/4 tsp dried basil

1. In a small mixing bowl, mix all ingredients until well combined.

Drizzle over grain bowls, salads, and veggies, or use as a crudité dip.

Prep-ahead!

CREAMY DILL DRESSING

Ingredients
(yield ~3-4 servings)

- 1/4 cup hummus (can substitute for unsweetened yogurt)
- 2-3 tbsp water
- 2 tbsp finely chopped fresh dill
- 1/8 tsp fine grain salt

1. In a small mixing bowl, mix all ingredients until well combined. Add an additional tbsp of water if you would like a thinner consistency. Store in the fridge for up to 5 days.

Delicious drizzled over salmon or as a dip for veggies.

Prep-ahead!

DESSERTS

SALTED TAHINI COOKIE DOUGH

Ingredients (~2-3 servings)

- 1/4 cup room temperature tahini
- 1/4 cup vanilla protein protein powder
- 1/4 cup almond flour
- 1 tbsp coconut sugar
- 1 tbsp maple syrup
- 1/4 tsp cinnamon
- 2 tbsp white chocolate chips
- 1 tbsp coconut oil, melted and cooled
- 1/8 tsp fine grain salt

1. Mix well until all ingredients are combined.
2. Optional: Use a cookie scoop to form into a small jar or container (I sugared the rim with coconut sugar for serving).
3. Store in the fridge or freezer.

ALMOND FLOUR COFFEE CAKE

Ingredients (~6 small cake squares)

- Almond Cake:
    - 1 cup + 1/4 cup almond flour
    - 1/4 cup arrowroot starch
    - 1/4 cup coconut sugar
    - 1/4 cup maple syrup
    - 3 eggs, whisked
    - 1 tsp baking powder
    - 1 tsp vanilla extract
    - 1 tsp cinnamon
    - 1/8 tsp fine-grain salt
- Coffee cake crumble:
    - 3/4 cup oats
    - 2 tbsp coconut oil, melted
    - 1/4 cup maple syrup
    - 1 tbsp coconut sugar
- Optional Icing:
    - 1/2 cup powdered sugar
    - 1 tbsp nut milk
    - 1/8 tsp cinnamon
    - lower sugar icing option: 1/4 cup coconut butter + 1 tbsp maple syrup

1. Preheat oven to 350 degrees F.

2. In a medium-sized mixing bowl, mix eggs and add all other wet ingredients (maple syrup, vanilla extract). Then, slowly mix in slowly all your dry ingredients (almond flour, arrowroot starch, baking powder, salt, cinnamon, and coconut sugar).

3. Line a small baking dish or bread pan (6x4" approximately) with parchment paper. Add your almond cake mixture and smooth into an even layer. Bake for 28 minutes or until clean fork test is passed.

4. While your cake is baking, melt your coconut oil and mix all ingredients for the coffee cake crumble topping. Pop the crumble in the fridge for ~5 minutes so the coconut oil can set.

5. If you'd like to add the icing, mix your powdered sugar and nut milk (optional dash of cinnamon) until you have a thin icing consistency. You could also mix 1/4 cup coconut butter and 1 tbsp maple syrup here if you prefer to not use powdered sugar.

6. Once your cake is done, remove from the oven and allow to cool fully before carefully removing from your baking dish.

7. Top your cake with the coffee cake crumble and optional cinnamon icing. Slice and ENJOY!

NO-BAKE BERRY CHEESECAKE

Ingredients (~8 servings)

- 1 1/2 cup pecans
- 1 cup unsweetened coconut shredded
- 1 cup + 3 tbsp maple syrup
- 1/2 tsp salt
- 3 tsp vanilla extract
- 2 cups fresh or frozen berries of choice (I used frozen cranberries, but you can also choose strawberries/ blueberries)
- 2 cups raw cashews, soaked in filtered water overnight
- 1/4 cup coconut oil softened but not melted
- Juice of 1/2 a lemon

1. Line the bottom of an 8-inch springform pan or an 8-inch pie pan (like I used here) with parchment. In a food processor, pulse the pecans, coconut, 3 tbsp maple syrup, ¼ tsp salt, and ½ tsp vanilla until just combined but not pasty (may need to stop and stir). Transfer to your parchment-lined pan. Using wet hands, press firmly to cover the bottom and slightly up the sides of the pan to form a crust. Place the pan in the freezer. Wash and dry the food processor bowl.
2. In a medium saucepan, combine your berries and ½ cup maple syrup. Cook on medium heat for ~8-10 min, stirring occasionally until some berries begin to burst/breakdown. Remove from heat and allow to cool completely, then add to a bowl and refrigerate.
3. Rinse the soaked cashews and dry them thoroughly with a towel. Place cashews in food processor, along with the coconut oil, lemon juice, remaining ½ cup maple syrup, remaining 2½ tsp vanilla, and remaining ¼ tsp salt. Process until very smooth and creamy, stopping and stirring occasionally. Pour the mixture over the crust. Pop in the fridge for at least 1 hour. Before serving, spoon your stewed berry mixture on top.

WHITE CHOCOLATE COCONUT COOKIES

Ingredients (~14-15 cookies)

- 1 cup unsweetened shredded coconut
- 1/4 cup coconut oil, melted and cooled
- 1 egg
- 1/4 cup maple syrup
- 1/4 cup oat flour
- 3 tbsp arrowroot flour
- 1/3 cup white chocolate chips
- 1 tsp vanilla extract
- 1/2 tsp baking powder
- 1/4 tsp salt
- 1 tsp hemp seeds *optional, for topping

1. In a medium bowl, mix your liquid sweetener, coconut oil, vanilla, and egg. Then add all other ingredients (oats, shredded coconut, arrowroot flour, salt, baking powder). Lastly, stir in white chocolate chips.
2. Use a cookie scoop to form small even balls (~1.5") and lay on a parchment-covered baking sheet. Press the balls down with a spoon (or wet hands) to make a cookie shape.
3. Bake for 10 minutes at 350 degrees F. Remove and allow to cool fully before moving. Optional: Sprinkle with more hemp seeds and a touch of sea salt.

WHITE CHOCOLATE PUMPKIN PILLOWS

Ingredients (~12 cookies)

- 1 cup almond flour
- 2 tablespoons arrowroot starch
- 1/3 cup coconut sugar
- 1/3 cup pumpkin purée
- 1 egg, whisked
- 2 tbsp tahini
- 1/2 tsp vanilla extract
- 1/2 cup white chocolate chips
- 1/2 tsp baking powder
- 1/8 tsp fine grain salt
- optional glaze: 1/2 cup powdered sugar + 1 tbsp nut milk
- low sugar glaze: 1/4 cup coconut butter

1. Preheat oven to 350 degrees F. In a medium bowl, mix all wet ingredients (tahini, vanilla extract, pumpkin and egg). Then mix in slowly all other dry ingredients (almond flour, arrowroot flour, coconut sugar, chocolate chips, salt, baking powder). Lastly, stir in white chocolate chips.
2. Use a cookie scoop to form small even balls (~1.5") and lay on a parchment-covered baking sheet. Press the balls down with a spoon (or wet hands) to make a flat cookie shape.
3. Bake for 10 minutes at 350 degrees F. Remove and allow to cool fully before moving. If you'd like a glaze on the cookies, feel free to mix glaze ingredients and drizzle on top.

WHITE CHOCOLATE STRAWBERRY CAKE BITES

Ingredients (~8 bites)

- 3/4 cup oat flour
- 1 tbsp coconut sugar
- 3 tbsp maple syrup
- 1/4 cup room temperature tahini
- 1/3 cup white choc chips (+ additional 1/3 cup for topping)
- 1/3 cup freeze-dried strawberries, crushed (+ additional 1/4 cup for crumbling on top)
- 1/16 tsp fine-grain salt
- 1 tsp vanilla extract

1. Simply combine oat flour, maple syrup, tahini, salt, cinnamon, and coconut sugar ingredients until you get a thick dough that sticks together, but not to your hands. Then mix in your white chocolate chips and freeze-dried strawberries.

2. Form small even balls with a cookie scoop. Place on parchment and freeze for about 1 hour.

3. Melt the remaining 1/3 cup white chocolate chips in the microwave for 60-90 seconds and pour 1 tsp melted chocolate over each truffle. Sprinkle with crushed freeze-dried strawberries for added color and pizazz!

SINGLE-SERVE BERRY CRUMBLE

Ingredients (1 serving)

- Berry base Ingredients:
    - 1/4 cup frozen blueberries
    - 1/3 cup frozen raspberries
    - 1 tbsp coconut sugar
    - 1/2 tbsp arrowroot starch
- Crumble topping ingredients:
    - 3 tbsp whole oats
    - 1 tbsp almond butter
    - 1 tbsp coconut sugar
    - 1 tbsp coconut oil, melted
    - 1/4 tsp cinnamon
    - Dash of fine-grain salt

1. Grab a small bowl and combine the berry base ingredients together (berries, coconut sugar, arrowroot starch). You can use any berries here (or even sub for 1 diced apple if desired). Add this mixture to a small oven-safe bowl.
2. Mix the crumble topping ingredients (oats, almond butter, coconut sugar, coconut oil, cinnamon, and salt) until well combined. Top over your berry mixture.
3. Bake for 23-35 minutes. Remove from the oven and sprinkle with hemp hearts or top with yogurt or ice cream.

GINGER BREAD DONUTS

Ingredients (~4-5 donuts)

- 1 1/4 cup almond flour
- 1/4 cup molasses
- 3 eggs, whisked
- 1 tbsp coconut oil, melted
- 1 tsp cinnamon
- 1/8 tsp ground clove powder
- 1/8 tsp fine-grain salt
- 1 tsp baking powder
- Glaze: 1 cup powdered sugar + 2 tbsp nut milk, OR 1/4 cup coconut butter + 1 tbsp maple syrup

1. Preheat oven to 350 degrees F. In a large mixing bowl, combine eggs, coconut oil, and molasses. Then slowly add all dry ingredients (almond flour, baking powder, cinnamon, ground clove). Mix until combined.
2. Spray or grease a silicone mini donut mold with avocado oil or coconut oil. Distribute the mixture to the molds, filling the molds 3/4 of the way up. Bake for 18-20 min at 350.
3. Remove and allow to cool fully before removing from molds. Mix your icing (you can choose to use powdered sugar or coconut butter) and drizzle on top.

CINNAMON SUGAR BANANA BREAD DONUTS

Ingredients (~6 donuts)

- Wet Ingredients:
    - 2 super ripe bananas, mashed
    - 2 eggs, whisked
    - 1 tbsp coconut oil, melted
    - 1 tsp vanilla extract
- Dry ingredients:
    - 1 1/2 cup almond flour
    - 2 tbsp arrowroot starch
    - 1.5 tbsp cinnamon
    - 1 tsp baking powder
    - 1/8 tsp fine-grain salt
- Cinnamon sugar coating:
    - 1/4 cup coconut sugar
    - 1 tsp cinnamon

1. Preheat oven to 350 degrees F. In a medium-sized mixing bowl, mash bananas and mix all wet ingredients (eggs, coconut oil, vanilla). Then slowly add the dry ingredients (almond flour, arrowroot starch, baking powder, cinnamon, salt). Mix well.
2. Grease your donut mold with avocado or coconut oil. Fill each donut mold with your banana bread mixture.
3. Bake for 20-22 min. While they are baking, mix the ingredients for the cinnamon sugar coating on a small plate for dipping.
4. After 18-20 minutes or when the donuts have passed the clean toothpick test, remove from the oven. Allow to cool fully before removing from your mold (very important). Dip the top of the donut into your sugar-cinnamon mixture. Store in the fridge for up to 5-6 days.

REFLUX-FRIENDLY RICE CRISPY TREATS

Ingredients (yields ~4-5 treats)

- 1 1/2 cups puffed rice, or puffed quinoa
- 1 cup sunflower seed butter
- 1/3 cup maple syrup
- topping: 1 cup white chocolate chips + 1 tbsp melted coconut oil

1. In a large mixing bowl, simply combine the puffed rice, sun butter, and maple syrup. Press your mixture into a small parchment-lined baking dish (~4x4") to form a condensed, thick 2-3" layer. Pop in the freezer.

2. Melt the white chocolate over a double boiler or in the microwave for 60-90 seconds. Mix with 1 tbsp melted coconut oil and pour the white chocolate/coconut oil mixture onto your crispy layer. Optional: sprinkle with a dash of cinnamon and sea salt. Freeze for ~1 hour.

3. Remove and allow to sit on the counter for 10 minutes before slicing with a hot knife (run under hot water to heat). Store in the freezer or fridge.

MINI COCONUT MACAROONS

Ingredients (yields ~12-14)

- 1 large egg white, room temperature
- 1 tsp vanilla extract
- 1/4 cup coconut sugar
- 1 cup unsweetened shredded coconut
- 1/8 tsp salt
- optional icing:
    - 1/2 cup powdered sugar + 1 tbsp nut milk or water
    - lower sugar option: 1/4 cup coconut butter

1. Preheat the oven to 325 degrees F and line a baking sheet with parchment paper.
2. In a medium bowl, whisk the room temp egg white until it begins to turn frothy (~3 min). Then, mix in vanilla extract, sugar, and salt. Lastly, mix in the coconut until thoroughly combined.
3. Use a small cookie scoop or spoon to drop mounds of the coconut mixture onto your baking sheet. After forming all of the cookies (about 12-14), wet your fingers into warm water (to prevent the mixture from sticking to your fingers) and gently pat/reshape each mound into a more spherical shape.
4. Bake at 325 F for 22-24 minutes, or until the macaroons are golden to your liking. Allow to cool completely before moving or drizzling with icing.

SNICKER DOODLE COOKIE DOUGH BITES

Ingredients (~8-9 bites)

- 1 cup oat flour
- 2 tbsp maple syrup
- 1/4 cup room temperature tahini
- 1 tsp cinnamon
- 1/16 tsp nutmeg (optional)
- 1 tsp vanilla extract
- 1/4 tsp salt
- snickerdoodle coating:
    - 1/2 tsp cinnamon
    - 3 tbsp coconut sugar

1. Mix all ingredients well until you have a thick dough that sticks together, and not to your hands.
2. Form small balls with a small cookie scoop or tablespoon. Gently roll the bites in your hands until smooth and round.
3. Mix together cinnamon and coconut sugar for snickerdoodle coating and pour on a small plate. Now, gently roll bites in the snickerdoodle coating until covered in a light dusting. Store in the fridge.

I'D LOVE YOUR FEEDBACK

[SCAN ME QR code]

LEGAL

All content within this package is © Molly Pelletier 2022. All rights reserved. No part of this publication may be reproduced, transmitted in any form or by any means, electronic, mechanical, photocopying, recording or otherwise, without prior written consent of the authors.

This publication contains the opinions and ideas of its author and is to be distributed for educational purposes only. It is sold with the understanding that the author, Molly Pelletier, is not responsible for the use or misuse, or consequences resulting from the information or suggestions described in this package This package is not to be substituted for professional medical advice, diagnosis or treatment.

Disclaimer: The information in this book/meal plan is in no way prescriptive and does not intend to replace medical advice, psychological advice, or personalized Nutrition Therapy. The reader assumes full responsibility for consulting a qualified health professional regarding health conditions or concerns, and before starting a new diet/exercise/wellness program. Molly Pelletier and accompanying social media are not responsible for adverse effects/reactions resulting from the use of any recipes, plans or suggestions herein or procedures undertaken hereafter. If you are experiencing gastrointestinal discomfort/symptoms, have a medical condition, food allergy, or history of an eating disorder, please seek help from a qualified medical professional.

© Molly Pelletier 2022

REFERENCES

1. Taraszewska A. Risk factors for gastroesophageal reflux disease symptoms related to lifestyle and diet. Rocz Panstw Zakl Hig. 2021;72(1):21-28. doi:10.32394/rpzh.2021.0145
2. Tack J, Pandolfino JE. Pathophysiology of Gastroesophageal Reflux Disease. Gastroenterology. 2018;154(2):277-288. doi:10.1053/j.gastro.2017.09.047
3. Surdea-Blaga T, Negrutiu DE, Palage M, Dumitrascu DL. Food and Gastroesophageal Reflux Disease. Curr Med Chem. 2019;26(19):3497-3511. doi:10.2174/0929867324666170515123807
4. Zhang M, Hou ZK, Huang ZB, Chen XL, Liu FB. Dietary and Lifestyle Factors Related to Gastroesophageal Reflux Disease: A Systematic Review. Ther Clin Risk Manag. 2021;17:305-323. Published 2021 Apr 15. doi:10.2147/TCRM.S296680
5. Fujiwara Y, Machida A, Watanabe Y, et al. Association between dinner-to-bed time and gastro-esophageal reflux disease. Am J Gastroenterol. 2005;100(12):2633-2636. doi:10.1111/j.1572-0241.2005.00354.x
6. Naliboff BD, Mayer M, Fass R, et al. The effect of life stress on symptoms of heartburn. Psychosom Med. 2004;66(3):426-434. doi:10.1097/01.psy.0000124756.37520.84
7. Cho YK. Can Acute Stress Cause Esophageal Hypersensitivity in Healthy Individuals?. J Neurogastroenterol Motil. 2017;23(4):483-484. doi:10.5056/jnm17118
8. Eraslan D, Ozturk O, Bor S. Eating disorder symptoms improved by antireflux surgery: a case report with a six-year follow up. Isr J Psychiatry Relat Sci. 2009;46(3):231-235.
9. Cherpak CE. Mindful Eating: A Review Of How The Stress-Digestion-Mindfulness Triad May Modulate And Improve Gastrointestinal And Digestive Function. Integr Med (Encinitas). 2019;18(4):48-53.
10. Livovsky DM, Pribic T, Azpiroz F. Food, Eating, and the Gastrointestinal Tract. Nutrients. 2020;12(4):986. Published 2020 Apr 2. doi:10.3390/nu12040986